g02597

Northern Latitudes

Northern Latitudes

Prose Poems

Lawrence Millman

THE
MARIE
ALEXANDER
POETRY
SERIES

New Rivers Press
2000

First Edition
Library of Congress Control Number: 00-105588
ISBN: 0-89823-207-4
Edited by Robert Alexander
Cover: *Greenland Winter* by Rockwell Kent. Courtesy Jake Wien
Series design and typesetting by Percolator
Printed in Canada
The Marie Alexander Poetry Series, number 3

The publication of *Northern Latitudes* has been made possible by support from Robert Alexander; the Minnesota State Arts Board (through an appropriation by the Minnesota Legislature and the National Endowment for the Arts); the McKnight Foundation; and the contributing members of New Rivers Press.

NATIONAL
ENDOWMENT
FOR THE
ARTS

MINNESOTA
STATE ARTS BOARD

New Rivers Press
420 North Fifth Street Suite 1180
Minneapolis, MN 55401

www.newriverspress.org

Author's Note

———

Northern Latitudes can be read as a lyric record of my travels in the North between 1975 and 1999. Since I visited them, several of the places I refer to have adopted new names; for example, the eastern portion of the Northwest Territories (N.W.T.) is now the Inuit territory of Nunavut. In virtually every instance, however, I've retained the older name at the expense of the newer one because it is either more familiar, more colorful, more historically accurate, or more in keeping with the style of the particular piece.

This book belonged to my mom,
Elizabeth (Betsy) Barton.

It was one of 2,631 books that she treasured and left behind when she passed away in August 2024. Now I'm sharing her collection through Little Free Libraries across the country.

Inside you'll find a postcard - I'd love to hear a story about your own mom, or why you chose this book. I'm eager to connect with people who shared her interests!

Found a book but no postcard?
You can still share your story at
www.betsysbooks.com.

Every reader adds a new chapter to the story. I look forward to hearing from you!

~Sarah

 SCAN ME

Contents

I. Text Dwellers

II. Aurora Borealis

III. In the Westfjords of Iceland

I
Tent Dwellers

Bush Flight

The whimsies of wind and weather anchor me to a waiting room not much bigger than a closet. At last the wind dies down, but a thick overcast still hugs the horizon. On the wall is a dog-eared, out-of-date calendar, and having little else to do, I study it until I know last April intimately. How long have I been grounded in this forlorn box of a room? Since last April? My destination in the back country seems beyond my reach, or at least beyond the reach of a single-engine Cessna. At one point the ceiling lifts, and the pilot walks out to his plane. The ceiling lowers again, and he returns with a shake of his head. "Maybe in the afternoon," he says. But in the afternoon the ceiling is even lower, and the wind comes back with a vengeance. At the doorway I listen to the howling world, and after a while, notice a speck of sunlight dimpling the sky like a birthmark. Suddenly a dark curtain of clouds erases the speck. "Maybe tomorrow," the pilot says, then heads for home. After he leaves, the sky starts to brighten and the bullying wind subsides. I watch other planes take off for parts unknown.

Herschel Island Drift Logs

As if from the sea's catacombs come dearticulated bones, the shuttle of giant drift logs to these treeless shores. They're here by the hundreds, each etched with intricate hieroglyphs, the scrivening of worms, and each shellacked to smoothness by the frigid fingers of the Beaufort Sea. The most recent are chestnut brown, as yet undone by the high latitude sun, while the oldest have turned a friable gray. And on gray shingle they lie, a geometer's dream, askew, isolate, or piled high, as if to say, "We're just passing by."

Herschel Island Church

Squatting among tussocks of sedge grass, the dead boards of a church. Collapsed windows, permafrost floor, a fruiting of mushrooms in the nave, and a few astonished lupines at the door. An old British Admiralty Arctic Chart tacked to the wall. Yet what better place for divine worship? In the rotting rafters sits the congregation—a group of black guillemots. Day and night they proclaim their faith by singing high-pitched hymns of praise to the gaping solitudes. Their droppings decorate the ruined pews with intricate white scatter-patterns. Read these patterns, traveler, and you too might find deity.

Herschel Island: Inuit Graveyard

A scattering of crippled coffins pushed up by the permafrost   some
host a motley of moss-ridden bones, others only a brown-stained
skull, occiput, or toothless jawbone   there's a rib cage with the husk
of a snow bunting's nest splayed across it   occasional tufts of cloth
cling to an otherwise naked femur   if you return these coffins to the
ground, up again they'll rise   to be whipped by the wind, lord of the
oldest keening, or ogled by briefly mortal eyes   whipped and ogled,
whipped and ogled   until both coffins and their cargo of bones
translate into dust   out of which a lone immaculate arctic poppy
may one day grow

Faeroe Islands Courtship

For William Heinesen

It began in the usual fashion: no flowers. Instead they told each other ghost stories. He arrived at her island and told her about the drowned sailors who'd followed him on his journey there. She visited his island and announced that a ram's-headed succubus nightly invaded her sleep. That's sweet, he said, but just the other day I was grabbed by a hairy-faced troll and thrown into the sea. Hearing this, she offered him a cup of tea, then told a tale of time-honored gore about skeletons with sabers from Kirkjubøur. He told her of a ghost he knew who stole children aged three and under. She mentioned something green and putrefying that inhabited the old Torshavn churchyard. At this he shrugged. Hadn't he exchanged pleasantries with this same putrefying thing on a recent Sunday evening stroll?

So they got married and lived happily ever after.

Tent Dwellers

―――

Okak, Labrador

Inside this licheny ring of stones that once held down a sealskin tent, I pitch my own domed aquamarine tent and then quickly crawl inside to escape an ice pellet shower, whereupon I see a couple of my predecessors squatting dim and hazy, Dorset People with cupreous, epicanthic faces, scrapers of skin, tellers of tales, diviners of the weather, who stare at this pallid specimen from a distant age in his nylon-lined apparel, astonished that he somehow survived and they did not.

Cree Elder, Drunk

Wemindji, Quebec

Only a man like him who grew up with hardly a nudge from missionaries Catholic or Anglican and neither sugar nor spice from the Hudson Bay Company trader can know that when he pisses skyward in a vigorously rising trajectory the long yellow stream will reach all the way to the moon and illuminate it

Tundra

———

Near Ferguson Lake, N.W.T.

Here in this unadorned geology there's no getting away from last things. Several miles from my tent I find a caribou skeleton with its girders caved in, innards gone, and only a few forlorn tags of fur and skin to indicate that it wasn't born this way.

But then I see a few black flies hovering around the carcass like artists admiring their handiwork. In the dying wind I watch these few begin to multiply. All at once the air possesses an unnatural stillness. The sky seems to turn yellow, then a pocked, insectual black. And then these ravening lords of the tundra strike, mobbing my every available pore and drinking from my fountain. Each bite—not painful, but worse—sends a sharp pinprick of torment straight to the kernel of my bodily being.

I sprint off over broken ground, over esker and glacial rubble, lateral moraine and terminal moraine, heading in the direction of my tent. Rock after hard rock my feet waken from an early Pleistocene sleep. I plead with my Maker: I'll give up anything, Maker, Old Chap, sloth and gluttony, maybe even lust, only please, *please* deliver me from this plague of insects. There's no response except a thrumming acceleration of interest from the plague itself. Either God's bailiwick does not extend to these lovely abysmal parts, empty, powerfully empty of human habitation, or He shies away from encounters with rival lords.

Now I leap rivulets and splash through shoaly ponds, slop across bogs and tromp *tripe de roche*, until I reach, at last, long last, my glorious tent. Which, ingloriously, is nowhere to be seen. So again I splatter, plunge, hop, tramp, and slosh until I locate the tent in its rightful place a few feet from a riverine embankment. Cheek by jowl with a dwarf pillow patch. Not far from an ancient kayak stand. Surrounded by a bumper crop of Labrador tea. Except it isn't there again.

———

Where's the north wind when you really need its vindictive keen? My weary feet crunch a sedge meadow inlaid with a handsomely stitched tapestry of jewel lichen, but I'm far too fly-besotted to appreciate it. By now my morale is wholly unstrung, and I'm feeling the onset of histamine shock. Just give up, I tell myself, and let them drink their fill . . .

All at once I see the aquamarine dome of my tent in the distance. I run to it, trip, fall, rise again, and crawl inside, my own girders still aloft (barely). Then I quickly anoint my body with the magic of citronella oil and carbolated Vaseline, a dope guaranteed to distinguish my fate from the fate of my late caribou brother.

By such thin coatings we live and die.

Woman on the Ice

Ilulissat, Greenland, 1912

At Arnatsiq's death feast there was much talk about distant time. Five baby girls and two baby boys I threw in the snow, the old woman observed. Two others, twins, I drowned.

White Men would call you a murderer, her eldest son said. Added another son: White Men know only how to be too many. Nowadays they seem to be sitting on every stone from Ilulissat to Qaqortoq.

The next morning her eldest son led her from the feasting house to the cliffs. The sun was bright, snow and ice glistened like a carpet of gemstones. It was a beautiful day to die.

Push! she exclaimed.

Eldest son pushed his mother over the cliff. Down she tumbled, onto an ice mountain many feet below. Every bone in her ancient body broke. Her stomach and bladder broke. Her nose vanished from her face.

But she did not die.

And it was such a good push, too, she lamented.

The ice held old Arnatsiq all through the night. The next night as well. It held her as a husband might hold her, so she stung it with her tongue: Why do you refuse to give me my death, good-for-nothing?

The ice did not seem to hear her. It floated out the fjord, into the open sea. It floated away from the mountain where great-assed Erdlaversissoq welcomes guests to the other world.

Her father and mother visited her. We're waiting for you, daughter, they said. Why will you not come?

Because this ice won't let me, she told them.

Well, the drum cannot be beaten for you much longer, they told her. Its skin will break, and you know what that means.

Yes, I know. Eternal cold.

Then the Northern Lights Children danced with their afterbirths across the sky, singing, Join us! Join us!

I wish I could, Arnatsiq sighed.

One evening she saw a dark shape moving near her. It was the size of an ice mountain, yet it didn't appear to be an ice mountain. Perhaps it was a *tupilaq,* all bone and gaping jaws, intent upon tormenting her even more.

Then she saw *Titanic* written on it in big letters. A White Man's word. Maybe the word meant: We are too many. Maybe the dark shape itself was the vessel in which White Men got rid of their too many. She did not know. Did not care. She just wanted her death.

All at once there was a great jolt. Old Arnatsiq's ice mountain flung her into the arms of the sea. She sank down, far down, and never breathed air again.

At last I am content, she said to herself.

Spoken Cree: A Primer

For Jimmy Mianscum

waamistikushiish minhiikwaapaaiiyuu upishtikwaayaaukaamikw
paakumshumwaashtikw chisaawaamistikushiiu askwaapsuaanuuts

    if you wish to pronounce these words correctly, you must stick an old, very old piece of bear meat in your mouth, then chew with the fervent teeth of a carnivore, chew as you've never chewed before, and at the same time sing of goose hunts and moose hunts, fish weirs and ptarmigan snares, muskrat skulls and beaver balls, oracle bones and fire-making stones, maybe even include several lines of "Born to Be Wild" or "Going Up the Country," but not, definitely not, "Hotel California"—chewing and singing until the meat tastes as fresh as the north wind, and that's when you swallow it

Greenlandic Guesthouse

In the kitchen is a dead seal, its flippers like futile baby hands . . . the odors of fat and offal assail your nostrils from every room . . . the chamber pot is broken . . . the wind blows through the windows like the revenge of every kayaker drowned in these fjords . . . there's a bearskin drying in the bathtub . . . the next-door neighbors, remarks your landlady, are *inuittunit* (cannibals) . . . then she points smilingly to your sleeping space on the floor . . . you settle down among the meat scraps and bones of indeterminate animals . . . dogs howl, the wind howls, perhaps even some ghosts are howling too . . . you sleep the sleep of the blessed

Storyteller

For Marty Connor

You will know him by his capacious beard, home to warble flies, lemmings, louseworts, hairy butterworts, jaegers, rock tripe, bloodspot lichen, dwarf scouring rushes, boluses of musk ox shit, and (of course) mosquitoes. For nothing alien is alien to him. If the bubonic plague were to ask for a shakedown in his beard, the storyteller would say: "Come on in, old fellow. Always room for another outcast."

Laired among glacial erratics, sort of an erratic himself, he wanders the tundra in search of old bones. Such a splendor of them lying around. He picks up a femur here, a scapula here, a caudal appendage there, and in that clump of moss campion — what luck! — a nice little rib end. And having neither cellar nor attic, he puts his bone collection in the recesses of his own memory.

And now these bones, tucked away like children, await the day when they will be lashed together with the rock tripe and the flies, the lichen and the louseworts, and maybe even the occasional human being. Then they will all rise up as one and thank the storyteller for his paternity. Whereupon he will fluff his beard and remark: "It's nothing. Nothing at all."

Marble Island

Old Woman (the Inuk said) she left to die here many long agos. And when she does die, she turn into all rocks you see, all around island, even very small rocks. She a god maybe, or some kind of *tornraq*. You must crawl when you get out of boat, all the way up there, where the tide stops

What happens if I don't crawl?

Old Woman will kill you. Within a year and a day, but most of time just a couple weeks. Go away, go to America, doesn't matter, she follow you there. Maybe eat out your liver. Because you do not crawl ashore

But why crawl? Couldn't I just bow to her when I step ashore? Or leave her some sort of offering?

No good. Even money no good. Only crawling good. Because when you crawl, you kiss rocks with your body and that show you respect her. Kiss rocks, that important, most important thing of all

Raven Wife

Heard on Baffin Island

It was the same old story: a husband and wife were quarreling. Her tongue was sharper than a harpoon point. He would stab her legs with broken mussel shells. At last she went to an *angakok* and said, "Change me to some other creature, anything but a woman." He changed her into a raven. Now she flew off into the mountains and married another raven. But she kept returning to her old home at night. She would fly around it, waiting for a glimpse of her husband. "Oh, I wish he would come out and ease his bowels," she'd say to herself. Night after night she'd fly around, waiting for him. Then one night he did come out to ease his bowels. She flew down, saying, "What lovely shit you have, my husband!" At that moment she turned back into a woman, whereupon her husband took her for his wife again.

Iglulik Notes

_____

2:20 A.M. Here, two hundred miles north of the Arctic Circle, the bright red yolk of a sun sets, and a giant refreshed, immediately rises up again twice as robust as before.

"I ate human flesh maybe sixty years ago, when I was starving," the wattle-necked Inuk tells me, adding: "It tasted like inferior polar bear meat."

Locals say: The bearded seal is smart as a whip, and when it's harpooned, it becomes so indignant at being outwitted by a human being that it tries to claw out its eyes.

Inuktitut: a language of half-swallowed gutturals, semi-hisses, susurrations, clicks, and pops that sounds just like the sea ice cracking underfoot.

Ijjujut is the word for Bible, and *igujut* the word for testicles. So it is that the new minister, a *qallunaaq* (white person) poorly versed in the language, asks his congregation to pay more attention to their testicles.

Dwarf birches huddle together in the lee of a large rock, cowering before the eternal threat of winter.

The old man is wholly confounded by the *qallunaaq* notion of Heaven. For he can't believe that anyone would want to give up smoking, drinking, swearing, carousing, and venery for—what?—a pair of wings?

A silence so complete that it brings a whistling to the ears.

_____

East Greenland Notes

———

Tiniteqilaq: there was a man who got bored with his wife, so he ate her. As punishment, the village forced him to marry a certain widow, a bitter harridan and even more boring than the woman he ate. In his later years, the man was often seen crying at the grave of his first wife.

Grains of snow hard enough to draw blood — the fluffy stuff, by comparison, is an impostor.

The old man confides to me: lake monsters and even sea monsters don't bother him, but he's terrified of butterflies — those huge flapping wings!

Sea ice: a lunatic's labyrinth. There's no way out, and no way in. Leads form, then abruptly disappear. Boats can get frozen in for days, even weeks, vainly waiting for a shift in wind or weather. You can't help but admire something so wholly indifferent to human endeavor.

The height of fashion in Kulusuk—girls wearing diaphragms as necklaces.

East Greenlanders thought it was all right to murder someone if after murdering him you immediately ate a piece of his liver. But that was a long time ago, according to my guide. I ask him how long ago. Oh, thirty or forty years, he says.

Not a shred of pastoral softness, not a single errant fiber, no presumptuous trees or shrubbery, only the earth's scoured bones sticking up heroically.

Flowers: only fireweed, harebells, Lapland rosebay, and a few wads of arctic cotton. But each is a survivor.

———

It takes twelve years for polar bear shit to be broken down in these parts. It would take more than five hundred years for a candy bar wrapper to be broken down. God knows how long it'd take a TV, a computer, or a microwave. Perhaps never. Which makes you appreciate the polar bear shit all the more.

Grimsey

———

Weird gleams at midnight — the moon reflecting off the dead eyes of cod hung up to dry.

The eviscerated shark, tossed into the sea, snaps its jaws and begins devouring its own delectable innards.

Northwesterly gales blow all the time. Or almost all the time. Once, inexplicably, they stopped — so braced was I against the constant blowing that I nearly fell on my face.

A few months ago a polar bear wandered onto the island. A small boy thought it was a white horse and started petting it. The bear, appalled, returned to the sea.

We don't eat seal meat on Grimsey, the man says. For seals are descended from the Pharaoh's soldiers who drowned in the Red Sea while pursuing the Israelites. It'd be like eating, well, boiled Egyptian.

To shift one stone in this domain of stones would be like putting a fly on the wall of a Vermeer painting.

Near my tent, a single red *Amanita muscaria* mushroom peers forth from the gray basaltic ground as if embarrassed that it's not gray, too.

Geology is all.

———

A Little Night Music

———

Here I am, twenty-five miles west of Utshimassits, Labrador, answering nature's proverbial call in the middle of a winter night. It's so cold that I can hear tree branches breaking off and falling to the ground. The whistling wind pierces my anorak, supposedly windproof, and begins roaming along my bones like virtuoso fingers on a keyboard. My piss crackles on the hard snow, raising a delicate haze of steam. Overhead I watch the blue-green streams of the aurora open and close, open and close, like a celestial concertina. The stars are kicked-up flakes of snow, glistening pinpricks in the dark abyss of the sky. I gaze at them until the wind sings these words to my nearly numb flesh: now that you've answered your call, it's retreat or die. So back I go, half frozen yet fully blessed, back to my tent's cozy, life-giving unloveliness.

Winter Night

———

From the German of Georg Trakl

Snow's falling. Drunk with purple wine, you leave mankind's dark kingdom, the bright flame of human hearths, and begin climbing the blind minute hands that tick after midnight.

Black frost. The earth is stiff, and the air has a bitter flavor. Your stars conspire with evil signs.

With petrified steps you trudge along a railway embankment. Your eyes are the rounded, fearful eyes of a soldier storming a black bulwark.

Bitter snow and moon.

A red wolf strangled by an angel. Your legs clanking together like pieces of blue ice. A combination of grief and arrogance has turned your face to stone. Your forehead grows pale with the frost's lust.

You bow silently over the sleep of a watchman collapsed in his wooden hut.

Frost and smoke. A white shirt of stars burns your weary shoulders. God's vultures tear at your metallic heart.

O Hill of Stones. Cold and forsaken, your body melts away quietly in the silver snow.

Black, black sleep. For what seems like an eternity, your ears follow starry pathways in the ice.

Then the chiming of village bells awakens you. From the eastern gates appears the silvery-rose light of a new day.

———

Heimaey

Vestmannaeyjar, Iceland, 1/23/73

The night had made its covenant with seabirds and silence. The snow was stock-still in the sky like pluckings of wool stuck to a window. One by one the lights went out in the harbor. All at once the island shivered. The sward in the fields was torn asunder and flung into the air. Pebbles leaped up as though someone had struck the ground from within. Then this ground bloated like a dead body. And cracked as if an invisible knife was being drawn along it. Lava oozed from the wound like blood.

It was a year of thirteen moons. In such a year, the old people told us, the world would come to an end. The Midgard Serpent would vomit a terrible poison into the air, and then the fire-giant Surtur would ride out with flaming brands that would lick heaven itself and outburn the sun.

Soon molten lava was cradling my farmhouse with its tributary fingers. And then it was rolling toward my fields, which fifty years I kneaded, stone by wayward stone. Every clod of earth I ever pushed before me all those adamant years—from the sky it came back, split into ten thousand shards of pumice and tephra.

The air itself was thunder. Suddenly my horse went berserk. She reared on her hind legs, teeth bared, eyes jerked white with terror. Her stride was a gallop in an instant, heading in the direction of the eruption. Cinders stuck to her mane, which soon became a welter of tossing flame. I last saw her blazing silhouette against the dark bulk of Helgafell.

For weeks, red skies lit up our nights. Whirling lava bombs targeted our homes and gutted them. We cleared the tephra from the remaining rooftops, it seemed, with our fingernails. But then the sea came to our rescue as it had many times before. For we fought the fire giant with seawater, which stupefied him, slowed and thickened and at last turned away all his poison.

It was a mercy that none of us was killed. But when the giant fell, he killed my fields. His broken vertebrae will always be my harvest, and his gray skeleton paved my haycrop. They say that the eruption gave us a better harbor and brought us cheap heat. Yet still I wonder: How deep beneath all this rock does my horse lie buried?

Storm

Utshimassits, Labrador

Big storm coming, says Shushebish, but I'm such a great hunter that I'll just whistle in its face.

Storm arrives. Black sky all over, screeching wind. Storm bites Shushebish. He waves his bow angrily at storm, saying, Who dares to bite a great hunter like me?

Storm bites him again. Again. Yet again. Shushebish slaps at it, but he can't slap enough. For the storm was no storm at all, but a sky-darkening cloud of mosquitoes.

Now mosquitoes cover him from head to foot. Mosquitoes cover even his bow. Mosquitoes drink Shushebish dry. At last only his bones are left.

Moral: Whoever you are, there's always a better hunter somewhere in the world.

II
Aurora Borealis

Arctic Mushrooms

Baker Lake, N.W.T.

gently nodding in the wind, they ask so little of this little-giving habitat . . . at least the morsel of it that wasn't washed away ten thousand years ago . . . they ask only for water's blessing on a sliver of soil or cushion of caribou moss . . . that's all it takes for Boletus, Cortinarius, or Lactarius to fruit here . . . and then assume a magisterial posture beside their ground-hugging, wind-snipped neighbors . . . frailty, they seem to say, is in the eyes of the beholder . . . we are the mighty redwoods and giant sequoias of the tundra . . . abandon us not to your impatient boot . . . for our tawny heads and moist bodies have a place in the world, too . . . we too owe our existence to an act of love . . . the threads of our mycelia engage the ground no less firmly than the stalks of your legs . . . it's just that we travel down the river of time with slightly quicker paddle strokes than you . . . come back tomorrow, for instance, and we'll be gone . . . and all the more beautiful because of it

Parliament of Ravens

Iceland, 1983

Late spring in the mountains. Seven ravens gaze down on the low-lying world, and their bristly yellow beaks point and gesticulate. Not sunlight but hauteur makes their plumage iridescent; and not the northerly wind but the notion of plunder swivels their sleek heads now toward one farmstead, now another: If the horizon should turn indigo with the promise of rain, we will travel to Straumness . . . if pinholes of light appear through the clouds, then we will invade Baer . . . no, Baer is seeded more by scree than by grass . . . On and on they croak in these hungry heights. For they are deciding (as with all legislators) which lambs to kill.

Snail

Porcupine River, Yukon

I pick up a small snail from the glacial mud. Antennae twitch slowly, almost painfully, twin compasses of vigilance. Soon my flesh is a snail's wayward journey, with a ribbon of slime joining hand to wrist, crease to crease, pore to pore. I gaze at this fragile crustacean, a lodestar for the mortal man in me. For I, too, wish to live sweetly with my own skeleton.

Glacial Erratic

———

For Elliott Merrick

All alone it stands, headpiece of the world, far from the teeming fellowship of moraine, rubble, or till. A palimpsest of gray-green lichen adds a scurflike skin to its patina of bad weather. Its neck is joined to the cold Labrador firmament by a harmony so slight as to seem nonexistent and yet so strong that nothing could break it, not even Atikwapeo the Caribou God. No other landmark graces these barrens, twenty miles wide from eyelid to eyelid, except this granite boulder balanced on scoured rock, deposited here by the last Ice Age. Pariah and bulwark, it is an example of how to hold on to the austere bounteous earth. Hold on, vagabond, or you'll perish.

Moon/Snail/Sonata

Newfoundland

I hoisted my anchor and raised the canvas and sailed off to a broken-down North Atlantic town. There I fasted on the precision of solitude. For hours or years, hard to say which, I'd sit and gaze at barnacles, trying to find one that was legendary. Occasionally I'd stick a finger into an anemone's soft ciliated slit — a destitute mating.

When I landed, I was all flotsam. Maybe a little jetsam, too. Then one moonlit night I went down to the sea. The sand had been exposed by the tide, and I could hear a low crustaceal breathing above the tumult of the waves.

I found myself walking among the barrows and sand collars of moon snails. I bent down and picked up one of the globular shells. The furrowed foot, sequined with sand, was twice the size of its thick ashen shell. In its slow writhing, it seemed like an archaic brain. Its scent was briny and seductive, like certain flesh.

The moon snail possesses a monolithic energy for shutting itself off. It will not leave home even to die. You can't see its secret parts, see all of it whole, while it's still alive. And so when I touched the snail's outstretched foot, it withdrew into its whorled sanctuary with a flush of hostile water. The operculum, a great brown eye, now stared me in the face: cheeky bastard, it seemed to say.

Here I was, a late Pleistocene trespasser in the demesne of a Triassic survivor. There was nothing for me to do but give back my moon snail to the cadence of the tides. So I put it softly down in the sand-edged foam, and it became a polished gem, a sapphire, the moment a wave rolled over its shell. See how nice I look (it seemed to say) without the benefit of your touch.

At daystart and under a sudden scudding of rip-toothed clouds, I raised my weather-lashed canvas again and set off to find another landfall. I was still flotsam, probably jetsam, too. But it did not matter. Nothing mattered now except the wind in my sails.

Fish

———

An adamant brown crust washed up onto banded Hebridean gneiss, it refused the sun's caress. The eyes were missing, stolen by gulls, and the rest of it resembled a tide-wrenched, time-hardened rag. The head was a honeycomb, filled with sand and pebbles. Viscera and scales were welded into an irrevocable armor. It had no genus or species, nor anything familiar by which to identify its long-lost physiognomy. Even the scavenging gulls seemed to have lost interest in it. But in its elemental ruin it had achieved perfection. There was great serenity in its absence of eyes. In that gouged surface, a total strength. If you were to touch its honeycombed body, the frayed stitching would offer you a rough neolithic satisfaction. Would call you back. And that in itself is a kind of honey.

Hoy Windsong

———

For George Mackay Brown

Wind is deity. Wind swells the empty dawn and shakes the heather with big gray song. Wind breaks riderless horses against the five black angels of Hoy. Beats down on brawny boulders. Whittles sea stacks into contours of desolation. Whisks across derelict fields thickly starred with charlock. Wind bequeaths to tarns and bog-pools the pulsing ripples that it might once have whipped over frieze coat and cap.

Howls and squawls and growls this deity morning and night, the unsleeping music of the Hoy watchdog. A mastiff at once giant and unseen, it stands stark sentry from the Kame to Ward Hill, from the somber perpendicular heights of the Too to the crumbling crofts of Rackwick. Guardian of lost places, it protects with the caress of its breath those dead hearths that once burned turf. Fends against gorse-less hair, groping hands, trespassing machines. And bites again and again at skin that stands alien in the cairned ground.

From every point of the compass clamors this dog. The northerly gale is its pibroch, the equinoctial gale its strathspey, the westerly gale its hornpipe. When its bellows go awry, it comes raging up from the sea in the shape of a bone-chilling easterly blow. It favors only seabirds. Fulmar. Guillemot. Petrel. Dotterel. Bonxie. Arctic skua. Puffin. Shearwater. Jaeger. Kittiwake. The great dog of Hoy scours the crags and licks splotched stones into eggs. Then licks the nestlings into flight. Licks them round and round with the weight of its love.

Defender of faith and feather, with the fierce touch of your tongue visit oh visit our own fallow islands as well.

———

Periwinkle Piece

Croque, Newfoundland

The periwinkle hovering over these sea-tumbled rocks puts me in mind of you, my love. I lost you in the mists and crevasses of a foreign season. There were oceans between us, and I could see you only in the troughs of my dim thalassic skull. Your soft auburn hair was stretched out Ophelia-like in the seaweed of my thoughts, although I was the one who was drowning.

But the periwinkle chews a narrow slit through the bladder of this seaweed and deposits its eggs, a viscid mass safe from the buffeting tide. Soon that mass will become hundreds of brittle lives, each trailing a near-invisible silver banner behind it. Those that survive will preserve pride of locality by seeking, perhaps finding, perhaps not, the same tangle of seaweed that wombed them.

I know you'll always be there, chewing away, hundreds of you chewing away at my memory. I'll be the abyss that feeds you. You'll draw your moisture from me, and I'll draw mine in steady buckets from the sea. Your skin will be the place where nothing happens. Even so, we will be together, always together, through the storms and death-rattle doldrums of our mutual seas.

Eider Duck

Grimsey, Iceland

Her husband is a dashing sort of fellow, with a rich velvety black crown and the low seductive voice of an oboe. His black wings with white coverts suggest a tuxedo or the fancy dress uniform of a navy admiral. But she's a paradigm of dowdiness, as unlovely an avian as you'll find on these not-necessarily-lovely shores. Her plumage is a vermiculated spinsterish brown. Bulky and thick-necked, she waddles wherever she goes. And when she takes off, she emits a greenish fluid that smells like rancid liver in a frying pan. What's almost as bad, she (uncomely sound!) quacks. Yet the brownish-gray down below her springy chest feathers will keep the world's abysmal cold away.

Musk Ox

Cambridge Bay, Victoria Island

Less than a hundred yards away he stands, huge, humpbacked, and primordial, a relict from the Ice Age bequeathed to the present age. His broad, skull-hugging horns are lethal, so I move toward him slowly. He continues to graze away shaggily on his patch of dwarf willow, so I move closer yet. And still this hirsute marvel, this extravagantly camouflaged goat, this early Pleistocene visitant ignores me. Whatever I am, I'm much less interesting than his willow browse. Now I creep even closer. Suddenly he jolts alert, startled by the crunch of my boots on glacial litter. Then off he canters in a cloud of kicked-up tundra and flying underfur. It isn't long before he's a small, remote speck against the wide horizon. And then he disappears from my life forever.

Shells

———

Newfoundland, 1986

clathrate trophon, flat-coiled skeneopsis, reticulate turret, great piddock, Largilliert's whelk, smooth velutina, double-sutured odostome, Couthouy's nutmeg, *Neputunea decemcostata, Cuspidaria glacialis, Colus ventricosa, Aporrhais occidentalis, Lacuna vincta, Epitonium greenlandicum, Lora nobilis*

Birds they were when all else was mire and millennial childhood. Back and forth they would fly across the old prodigal sky, voyagers in unflagging transit. But who can wrestle with the gravitational pull of earth? Who plundered felicity from the lyric heavens? As whales crept back to their aqueous beginnings, so these shells dropped from the shuffling clouds to the sullen depths of the sea. Their song turned into mother-of-pearl, octave of rainbow, and a nocturne of whorls. Their feathers became flesh pliant enough to envelop geology.

But sometimes very late at night I've seen them glide silently across the moon, testing their obsolete wings, shaking the sand from the grooves and corkscrews of their secret bodies.

Sea Cucumbers

Anticosti Island

Bags of lumpy vegetable skin grinding endlessly grinding at sediment . . . their cloacas inhaling and exhaling water nonstop to oxygenate their innards . . . they lie on a sea bottom littered with three hundred years of shipwrecks . . . they're no doubt a bit surprised at the presence of so much rotting timber . . . for sea cucumbers have never suffered any sort of shipwreck . . . never been deluded by a false light on shore . . . never had rough waters swarm their gunwales . . . and never gotten lost in fog . . . which makes you wonder who's savvy and who's not

Limpet

───

Where other snails possess fancy coiled shells, the limpet owns only a weathered coolie hat. Where others protect themselves with operculums, it must walk barefoot through the world. And where others emulate rainbows or prisms, its colors are dull brown or gray—the garb of a prisoner. At high tide it moves, but only for an hour, and then it must return to the rock that bears its outline, its scar. Yet this scar is the emblem of the limpet's salvation. So powerfully does it graft itself to the rock of its choice that not even a hurricane can dislodge it. Meanwhile, the tides sweep its elegant brethren ashore, and on rough shingle they die under the dazzle of the sun, their lovely colors fading, quickly fading away. To which the limpet seems to say: it isn't the clothing but the secluded flesh beneath that makes the emperor.

Sea Urchin Variations

———

Iceland, 1984

Beneath a cornucopia of spines meditates the sea urchin. *Noli me tangere* announce these nettlesome spines, each barbed at the tip. They are his escutcheon on the battlefield of the littoral/literal world. They protect him from the gaucheries of the merely curious. They keep his meditation intact. Spines, pentamerous lantern, cast, tube feet, and five-branched gonads—such is his bag of possessions. He needs nothing more.

Give him whatever sobriquet you like—Sea Porcupine, Sea Egg, or Whore's Egg. Give the Green Sea Urchin the scientific name *Strongylocentrotus droehbachiensis,* probably the longest Latin binomial in zoology . . . or give him a heartfelt expletive. Yet whatever you give him, the sea urchin will answer only to a higher call: the call not to answer.

The sea urchin yearns only to be as unremembered as his own ancestors. So he sequesters his body in stone. In stone, he repels the furious reckoning of the sea. In stone, he dines on pips of the perpetual dark. And in stone, he builds his home with five articulated jawplates that are soft as silk. How he manages this apparent contradiction he would not betray even to his confidant Aristotle.

Solipsism is the sea urchin's birthright. Query him about his hermetic habits, and he might defer to his sea star kinfolk . . . or to silence. Inquire about the reputed aphrodisiacal properties of his roe, and he'll shrug too intimately for the naked eye to see. Try a hands-on approach, and you'll end up with a hand full of spines. That's what you get (the sea urchin says) for attempting a dialogue with a solipsist.

Beneath a cornucopia of spines meditates the sea urchin. Back and forth, back and forth, these spines wave in the currents, not saying hello, but saying good-bye.

———

Aurora Borealis

jade-green, flame-orange string figures spanning the wintered-up sky . . .
legions of stillborn infants dancing back and forth with their after-
births . . . a wolverine's neon jaws snapping open and shut, open and
shut . . . the glistening hair of every woman ever simplified by death . . .
the ghost fires of long-dead hunters . . . spectral bears roaming the
heavenly tundra . . . sky dwellers kicking around walrus heads . . . sys-
tole and diastole of the great Moon Man

you are brighter, many times brighter, than the mundane sun

The Origin of Fish

———

From an Icelandic Folktale

Long ago the sea held no life but the blustery lives of its own drifts and frisksome eddies. Its waves beat the land and receded, leaving only idle spume in their wake. Then on the shingle of Borgarfjordur appeared three countrymen, each boasting a mighty wad of snuff in his mouth. The first, Jesus Christ, was a farm-bodied hogshead of a man with the fields of twenty cows. He spat into the fjord, and from his spittle came the halibut. Next was Saint Peter, who had twelve cows and a face like the mountainy rock of Snaefellsnes. He spat, and from this came the flounder. The third, Nick Fire-Breath, he of the cleft foot and sulfurous reek, was naught but a shepherd on Hjorsey, but he wished to show that he was as useful as the others. So he spat into the fjord, and from his spittle came the lowly jellyfish.

These three antique men are now dust, but the fish they fashioned live on in the generous waters of the sea.

———

Lichen

For Dick Smyth

May the gods of the tundra grant me lichen until I become lichen myself. Let me be a rich orange nitrophilous lichen tumbling like a fugitive spirit from the stones of an Inuit burial cairn. Let me, a foliose lichen, stitch otherwise naked granite into a tapestry. Or let me become map lichen so that I can possess my own geography. Or even let me be a patch of umbilicate lichen, crusty in my every skin. Grant me lichen, any sort of lichen, and I'll gratify your austerity. I'll survive on dust motes and the occasional drop of water, never complaining, never asking for more. Every hundred years I'll add an inch or two to my character. A millennium later I'll still lack all presumption. And still grasp the rock of my choice with a full-bodied embrace.

III
In the Westfjords
of Iceland

Mammoth

———

Porcupine River, Yukon

Somewhere far behind this olive-drab tusk protruding from a cut-bank is a mammoth munching on buttercups, an animal so big and robust and heroically woolly how could he realize that he's the last of his kind, that his brethren have all been made extinct by warm weather and improved spear points. So he just continues to munch away, and having eyes only for buttercups—ah! so succulent—he doesn't notice the hunters surrounding him until they thrust spears into his flank, and by then it's too late. Now they thrust those spears into his bulbous head, now his gut, now his great heart, whereupon he trumpets a brief astonished cry, as if to say, how in the name of all that's sacred could such trivial little creatures kill something like me, and then he tumbles to earth.

Sea Change

———

Deirdre Cunnane, age seventeen, drowned off
Inishbofin while gathering winkles

She grew up to be a great beauty, the gold of barley in her hair, handsome suitors at her feet. She drowned, wrapped in a tangle of kelp. Her father wished her alive and likewise wished her dead. Her only witnesses were the Stags of Bofin, the spring tide, and the mole-blue indolence of the sea.

Deirdre, oh Deirdre, you're the daughter I'll always dream on, all seven seas and a birth ago. You were rich in a skin that might once have grown old.

But she already knew this wisdom: that growing old would be the death of her. As it already was the death of each and every face in her own native place.

Father, there's a *ceilidh* in the sea tonight. May I wear my starfish brooch and my gown broidered by carrageen and maidenhair moss? And this once, just this once, may I come home late?

You may come home as late as you wish, my darling, he told her. You're a woman now as truly as the sea is salt.

She covered his words with her own flesh. Brewed up a rage for the squalid air of the West. She would give it oblivion and cherish the seawater that had always slipped through her girlhood fingers.

So downward she traveled, in a meander of porcelain bubbles, past goggly fish eyes and hairspun comb jellies, into the welcoming tentacles of the deep. How much easier it was to sink seawise than walk the whetted ribs of Bofin.

She came to rest on a soil as fine as flour — a soil so fertile that it seemed able to tickle itself to life. Here she needed neither plow nor harrow nor slane, just her own nautic body in its spume-filled gown. For whatever existed in this new liquid world existed in the swaying shape of a dance.

———

Her first partner was a graying old whelk with hardly more than a left foot to him. Next she suffered an Inishturk fisherman, long dead and dour, a hawser noosing his bony limbs. She did a slip jig with a dulse that was like a bout with sackcloth. Pushed to the surface, she ate the buttered bannock of the moon. And then she chose again: a lithe, bister-colored, long-muscled ribbon of kelp.

Her partner twined around her and clasped her, many times more vigorous than the men with brineless eyes she had danced with on land. The two of them moved nimbly like swans' necks swiveling around each other. She could not have found greater balm in the wind-stirred battlements above.

Father, may I marry? I wish to join myself to this kelp until the last calling of time.

You may, my darling, if that's truly what you want.

More than anything else in the world . . .

And the priest?

Drowned off the Stags two hundred years ago.

And so this father gave his daughter a blessing that did not come easy to him: Drown, my darling. Drown, drown, drown. Ease yourself into the embrace of the sea.

Which she did with all her heart.

She grew up to be a great beauty, the gold of barley in her hair, handsome suitors at her feet. She was never born, a child of mists and boulders, ever hidden in the fallow ground. Her father in the wintertime of his soul sired her looking seaward. He never once married, never dreamed again.

Tinker

Eyre Square, Galway

Of this drove of hygienic folk, his face alone offers a complete geography unto itself. It contains mile after mile of unpaved road—ruts, potholes, clefts, wheel marks. There are also loughs and drumlins and the evidence of persistent rain. Somewhere in this face the River Shannon flows. Yet the man does not suffer any known skin disease except that which rubs his skin against these abrasive times.

He is a scarecrow, arms suppliant, fingers like blackthorn roots. On his gaunt body hangs a ragtag frieze coat that looks centuries past its prime. Wherever he goes, you'd wager on a gathering of jackdaws or carrion crows. His few surviving teeth grow forward like the teeth of a grass-cropping animal. His cap is beaten flat and splayed over the pulleys of his ears, and his beard is a nest of thistledown, a wintered-out field of hay. His body purveys a medley of bog and sweat that might be the last strong odor in this cold Irish earth.

"Could ye spare a shilling, mister?" he asks. He seems to have forgotten that the shilling went out with the scythe and the slane, and with the tin pannikins he once peddled all through the lyric West. Now he peddles only his own ruinous person. And still he wanders, his only fuel a pint of porter. He wanders because he feels the turning of the earth and seeks to emulate it. Through Connemara and Mayo his itinerary winds like a tangle of snakes in the *Book of Kells.* He knows each lay-by and *boreen* from Tourmakeady to the sea. And he knows each guard by the cadence of his song—"Move on, move on." So move on he does, a memory incarnate, a visitant among small towns whose betrayal by the future makes them seem smaller yet.

St. Kilda Amen

Child of a sullen father, the Reverend John Mackay barked sermons to St. Kilda for a score of years. "Psalms are the ballast of heaven," he would say with trumpets in his voice. "No song but a psalm will sustain the thatch on your roofs. Balladry is a plague and a sin." And one by one the old songs would be lost at the fishing, on the steepdown cliffs, or among oats ground by quern.

Came a man Alexander Carmichael to copy down these songs. The reverend, invisible, cupped his palms to the mouths of man, woman, and child (and maybe even beasts in the field). His eyes burned at every window. At each hearth was silence or the muttering of prayer.

Neil MacDonald was hunting for a lost sheep, and he said this to a stone near Oiseval: "Why should I sing when there has been no wedding on our island for two years and a month? What would I sing of? I, son of Dugald, who has never lain with a woman? Son of Dugald, I have lain only with stones. For in my house, I live stone."

Calum MacQueen was gathering fulmars on the heights of Conachair, and he spoke these words to the horsehair rope that lowered him down the bird-fretted scarp: "My life is in your keeping, rope of Providence. Take me safely down these parlous crags. I will not cut your fibers with my unworthy voice." At the other end of this rope was Ruairi MacNeil. He took the fulmars sent up by his companion and put them in a hantle on the ground. He said this to the broken-necked birds: "For all your protests, you end up only in the salting cask. But you are not alone, my feathered ones: we are all perched on a ledge under Satan's watchful eye."

Anna MacNeil, wife to Ruairi, stood in ankle seawater and chipped limpets into the pouch of her raised skirts. Her boy Iain was beside her, and on his childhood lips she heard the beginnings of "All People That in Earth Do Dwell." She gave him a little clout. A sacred psalm (she told him) is not meant for the ears of crabs and limpets and sea urchins, beasties who serve an alien god.

Alisdair Ban MacKillop was shooting his nets to the maw of a storm when a wave pummeled him into the cold gray water. A fortnight later he washed up, gray himself, near Dun. His dead body spoke the time-honored language of the sea. His brother Finlay recognized the zigzag design of his pullover and said nothing but tears.

Near her eighth year to heaven, Christiana Gillies spoke these words to herself while plucking wool: "I am too young to know about songs. But often I have heard a knife in a sheep's throat. Is that the *oran mor,* the great song, which folk used to know? It sounds more like chapel on Sunday evenings, when the old people wear rags for voices."

The women at the quern once sang of courtships and heroic sea voyages, but now talked mostly of visitors: "Tomorrow arrives the *Dunara Castle* from Glasgow. I have twenty yards of tweed, three dozen stockings, scarves, gloves, and suchlike for sale. My little Morag has blown the eggs of thirty puffins. It will be a grand day, God willing." Visitors brought money to the island, and smallpox.

Each year the chill seeped deeper and deeper into Lachy Ferguson, so each year he shed a few bones and by that grew smaller, an old man with little that the weather could call its own. Piling peats into his hearth, he said this to the rising flame: "I've forgotten every song I ever knew except the song of warmth, and now I seem to be forgetting even that. May the eternal quiet of the grave grasp me soon."

But daft old Euphemia MacCodrum, alone in her dotage, sang a lullaby soft and clear to the child wrapped in the packet of her frailty. It was a seal child, a little selkie. The old woman sang these words: "It is time for me to leave you, my jewel, and to leave this place without tilth, for my home is far away, on Suleskerry. It is time and long past time, and a great grief will settle on me if I don't leave you now." So singing, and turning her eyes toward the sea, she began to unfasten such human flesh as the island of St. Kilda had granted her, revealing the seal beneath.

St. Kilda Mailboat

Great weather-faced cliff-climber Alisdair Gillies fashioned her from driftwood and the inflated bladder of a sheep. He carved a hollow into which he placed a small canister with this message etched in gannet quill: "Help send Doctor our Son Neil Gillies taken sick with the small-pox St Kilda December 19, 1897." Then near Laimhrig nan Gall he put her to sea. A moot of cormorants with lifted wings blessed her journey. Soon black waves were pushing at her strakes and hull. Two days she tacked and returned before a flood from the west swept her beyond the cleits and stacks of her native place. A northern squall whirled her proud wood mad. The hoof lash of breakers whelmed her narrow gunwales, and hailstones hammered her deck like cannonshot. But she came from a sainted isle. God in his everlasting mercy dwelt on St. Kilda. And God made the turbulent waters fall away from her keel like the Red Sea before Israel. A fair wind brought her in sight of the Cuillins of Skye. Swift and easy she passed the butt of Lewis, then tacked again, now southward, and made her landfall at Ness. There a crofter Murdo MacLeod retrieved her from the coarse shingle and slid open her hatch. Nothing was left of her message, licked by the hungry tongue of the sea, only vague purple loops of ink, scribblings from a long-lost alphabet. The crofter Murdo smashed her on the rocks and fired his hearth with her mutilated body.

St. Kilda Leavetaking

On that final sunshine morning   after which no fowler's hands would fondle the scarped cliffs of Mullach Sgeir   and the ferry lurked in the pearl-gray Bay of Hirta   the women of St. Kilda slowly came down the quay   looms strapped to their backs like crippled parents

Hence would they weave from alien sheep   their own fingers a strange-ness to them   for the artifacts straddling their bent backs   old bald wheel-heads and bony legs carved from the flotsam of the sea   would never again sing the same song   especially not in Scotland   where the bitter thistle grows

And of the last straggle of sheep   they fled to the high folds of Cona-chair   there they dined off each other's wool   grew a multitude of horns   and bore a race of fish-headed lambs   for when islands be-come derelict   O Lord   then will idiots rule the earth

Dream

Heard in Utshimassits, Labrador

Indian man he dream of good salmon fishing place on river, so he go there, sit down. One whole month he's sitting there, but catch no salmon. Only catch cold in chest. I'll take care of that damn dream, he say, and he bring big knife to sleep with him. So now dream comes again and tells him of another good fishing place. The man he stabs dream with knife, stabs again and again. Dream cries out, "You have killed me, stupid man," and dies. So now man does not even know where the bad fishing places are. He dies, too.

The Standing Stones of Callanish

If you gaze at them long enough, these stones will shake loose their lichen and dance in the blaffering wind. They will step through a Caledonian set that will freckle the shroud of night with stars. Come God, come Sunday, they will dance through the sulky streets of Stornoway. At the docks, pipers will celebrate their leaving. And then they will disappear across the Atlantic. To die heatherless. But if you gaze just a little while longer, they will walk slowly back to Callanish as if in a lament and bury their heads in the stony ground.

Ice Man: A History

Iglulik, N.W.T.

Inuk squatting beside a seal's breathing hole   harpoon poised in his
archaic hand   centuries pass   but he remains squatting in exactly
the same place   preserved by the cold   empires turn to dust   his
own descendants turn to dust   and still he squats there   a figure of
infinite patience   harpoon ready to strike   airplanes rip across
the sky   spacecraft land on the moon   satellites flit about the
heavens   but the man does not bother to look up   maybe he's think-
ing about his wife's *utsuuq*   or maybe just the seal's *aglu*   his gaze
does not waver from the hole   he does not move an eyelash   does
not even seem to breathe   waiting for the seal that will never surface

Child

Once upon an outworn Irish island twenty womanless men lived next door to the jostling elements. These men hungered for vague female hands to wring them dry from the mizzling rain; hands that would likewise steady them against ox-shouldered blasts of wind. They hungered for spuds sweetly boiled and whole-wheat dough sweetly kneaded, but drank instead the eternal bitter pint. By day they stood by the island's fretwork shore and awaited the boat by which something womblike might be borne westward to them. By night each man was a ghost who haunted himself with this refrain: "Please, God, save me from decency."

At last a man called the Fiddler wearied of lowering bent pin with bridebait to snag mermaids from the sea. So he elected, against all odds, to mate. He possessed a piercing wind-and-nettle knowledge of the physical land. But he didn't choose the land, which had been sucked thin and dry, and trodden to destitution by the thoughtless dead. And he didn't choose the sea (though living amaranth it was, sometimes), since the sea was far too big for a thewy little man like him. Instead, he took as his mate his own dappled mare. It was only natural, the others said. For hadn't he already mounted her thousands of times to and from the bog, turf in her panniers, fire in his hearth?

Some months later a foal-child was delivered of the Fiddler's mare. She stood trembling in her birth scent; she had rich satiny skin and amber hair and the head of a queen. She was the loveliest thing the twenty men had ever seen. All as one they climbed onto her mythic body and lightly kicked her flanks, and off they started for the land of their extinction.

Barra Crofter: Epitaph

There was a bullock that plowed the hardscrabble fields of this man's heart. There was a ewe ever ready to lamb in his infinite hands. He had frostflowers for eyes and brows of bracken and strips of heather for a beard. He could whistle in tune with gale-force winds. Then one year he grew thin as a bottled shadow; and the next year he cast aside his coil from too much western weather. He left behind this rich progeny: a winding of stone walls, a sheaf of thatch, a potato skib, two wooden noggins, three hob-lamps, a heap of dried turf, a rusty scythe, a sowing fiddle, a boot-shaped crub, a corn quern, and a centuries-black hearth. But the hungering mountains Ben Tangaval and Heaval rolled across his estate and claimed it for their own stony children. Rest in peace, old earth man.

Ronay of the Sorrows

Came the tall-masted shape of our end on Pentecost last. Dawn brought a *sluagh* from the west, will-o-the-wisps in the graveyard, and hissing voices that seemed to come from nowhere. Around our drinking well three heifers danced a circle. Our bullock burst into infant tears. Then the gale winds that ever rattle the sedge ceased, and we saw a ship that looked a mountain beside our own small luggers. We bade our women huddle together inside Saint Ronan's Chapel. We bade them pray.

Came the strangers among us who know the petrel's call more than the voices of men. They moored their ship at Geodha Stoth and oared their dory hard toward shore. We watched them stagger from tussock to furrow, as though, boat-born, they had suckled only the desolating dugs of the sea. Yet human creatures they were, swart gaunt-bodied seamen, clad in ganseys and ragged sarks. From twenty paces we could smell the brandy on their breaths. We could glimpse the fierceness in their foreign eyes. Even so, we readied for them vessels of milk and skin sacks of barley, as is our custom.

To these men we offered our soft Gaelic tongue
>> they replied in coarse-grained English
We blessed them walking sunwise
>> they mocked us by walking withershins
Mutton-gruel and dulse we set before them
>> like ravening beasts they ate
They said: "Three years in the Greenland fisheries"
>> we do not understand English
"Where are your women?" they said
>> we do not understand English.

Crofters of the short furrow, we possessed only bent-foot plows and these we knew how to wield only against the severe earth. The

Englishmen found our wives and daughters in the chapel and shamed them even inside it. Then they harried both stock and tilth, killed our sheep, and kindled the thatch of our roofs with brands from our own hearths. All of this we could suffer; all of this had happened before. But, great weft of our sorrow, they stole the bullock that was our pride and sustenance, our one and only bullock, the great bullock of Ronay. Already the chill of winter draws near, and the bitter rains.

A Prayer to Sean Ó Crochan
(1898–1975), Killed by a Lorry

———

Ballydavid, Ireland

May you whom the wheels of progress made one with Nineveh and Troy beam down on us benighted travelers from your celestial platter of spuds and forgive us our motorized trespasses through a land never intended by its rock-loving Creator to be traversed by any vehicle other than our own, our very own feet, which fit the ground perfectly, forever and ever, amen.

Blasketman

For Tom Biuso

Seaweed was your oakum, and the promontory of Blind Cove your curragh. For want of a few mackerel or pollack, you walked along sea-anointed rocks, feet in a lap of seawater, every day. Ahead of you The Three Sisters clawed the sea with eagle talons. At your back the Blasket was a dinosaur crouched to leap. Wind giants cracked their whips in your face. This island, this world, these rocks you called home.

As you walked, you gave a good whack with your mallet to each limpet, by which they knew you and stuck fast. You knew them as your bridge, your savior. Perhaps you were a limpet yourself in some former life. For you pitched your mortal tent on hard rock, and nothing would seem to dislodge you, not even the west wind.

In the mists of late October came your undoing. Did you leave your mallet lying in the sheep reek of your byre, or did you just trust to time-honored fate? Again you went down to the Cove, and now the limpets disowned you. They never guessed those hobnails belonged to you. For you were a force made of hammer blows dropped from on high.

And so you fell headlong into the cold Atlantic. The limpets sank too, stuck again, lived. But you could not swim. O Blasketman, you slipped into the green depths beyond the skin of the sea and entered new waters: ours.

The Last Angakok

Angmagssalik, Greenland, 1984

Bedridden he is, this bundle of age, who once could fly merely by flexing his index fingers. Songless he is, this man of songs, who once could chant away avalanches and *piteraq* winds with the great guttural of his voice. And full of sickness he is, this healer, who once could cure everything from rheumatism to possession by unfriendly spirits. Now there's no one left to cure him, and so his sleeping skins mark the compass points of his universe. Yet his eyes, slitted half moons, remain bright: they still inhabit a numinous realm. Flying is easy, they say. It's the not flying that's hard.

Beothucks

Croque, Newfoundland

Out of my brain's backcountry emerge three tall ochre-painted men dressed head to toe in deerskin. Their mocassins trip soundlessly through a frieze of black spruce and balsam fir, forest rubble and muskeg. At last, in the snow, always the snow, they arrive at my camp and squat down by the fire.

We are Beothucks, they declare in voices both close at hand and very far away.

But aren't you supposed to be extinct? I ask them.

Ah, extinction, one of them replies. It has its benefits.

Your fire cannot burn us, for instance, another says, and casually sticks his hand into the fire.

I gaze at them. Their eyes are crowberries squeezed into the swartness of their lost archaic faces. Their hair is slick with melted snow and littered with spruce needles, their fists like calcified chunks of suet. From their bodies emerge the savory smells of sweat, grease, and old campfires. Those bodies have a bearlike heft only the distantly dead seem to possess.

Now I offer them some of my dinner. Reconstituted chicken cacciatore. A far cry from fresh venison and tuckahoe, or moose nose smothered in rancid bear grease.

Thanks, but we don't need to eat anymore, they say.

Some tea, then?

We don't need to drink, either.

Well, is there anything you'd like?

Just a little of your time, friend. Where we come from, there's no time at all.

They stare into the crackling fire for a moment and then wander off into the universal snow, quickly gone from me, part of me gone.

In the Westfjords of Iceland

This is the ultimate place, a narrow inlet gnarled like a sheep's gut and blue glacial battlements sawed off down to the sea, all of a bareness and purity that will never riot into flower. Blades of quicksilver surf chisel to grit a shingle gray with the brains of basalt. Avalanches hurl a slow music at each other and board with boulders the windows of the earth. Everything is stone and adamant except:

The flotsam bones of birds. Tangled in the maidenhair of moss or strung up in fisherman's twine. Frail cages flexed to grotesque angles, as finespun as spider's floss. A bleached, open beak resting on a shakedown of dulse. A head with salt-widened eyeholes. Wingbones — torn from whose body? Stray feathers shiver in the east wind, and then with the north wind dissolve. All that remains is the delicacy of dismemberment.

These bones are the toys of extinction, my dear. Touch them. In this boreal place, grant them your small momentary warmth. Spread your fingers along their pale brittle surfaces. Untie the twine. Deliver these lost armatures of being from their obscure destiny. For it is only through your grasp that they will rise up and speak to you:

"We are the mad ones who haunt your comfortable night. Across every known sea we have journeyed so that you might witness us stripped bare of all decoration. We come from Babi Yar and Treblinka, from Rwanda and the extremities of sleep. We lost our wings in El Salvador and East Timor. In Auschwitz, our lords and masters washed their faces with the skin of our skin. In the Gulags, they bottled our breath in the frozen earth. But we have escaped such geography, jettisoned so much, that we might reach this fastness in the western fjords. Let not our travels be futile, my dear."

Acknowledgments

Some of the work contained in *Northern Latitudes* first appeared in *Agni Review, An Gael, Atlanta Review, Boston Review, Ceilidh, Che-Mun, Crosscurrents, Cutbank, Gaia, Greensboro Review, Mushroom, New England Review, Nimrod, Noh Quarter, North American Review, Northern Raven, Northwest Review, Paragraph, Penumbra, Terra Nova, and TickleAce.*

"Heimaey," "In the Western Fjords of Iceland," "The Origin of Fish," "Parliament of Ravens," and "Sea Urchin Variations" first appeared in the chapbook *Parliament of Ravens* (Loonbooks, 1986).

Lawrence Millman is the author of eight other books, including *Our Like Will Not Be There Again, Hero Jesse, Last Places,* and *An Evening among Headhunters.* His articles, reviews, stories, and poems have appeared in numerous magazines in the United States and Canada. He lives in Cambridge, Massachusetts.